Pork Recipes
8th edition

By Don Orwell

http://SuperfoodsToday.com

Your Free Gift

As a way of saying thanks for your purchase, I'm offering you my FREE eBook that is exclusive to my book and blog readers.

Superfoods Cookbook - Book Two has over 70 Superfoods recipes and complements Superfoods Cookbook Book One and it contains Superfoods Salads, Superfoods Smoothies and Superfoods Deserts with ultra-healthy non-refined ingredients. All ingredients are 100% Superfoods.

It also contains Superfoods Reference book which is organized by Superfoods (more than 60 of them, with the list of their benefits), Superfoods spices, all vitamins, minerals and antioxidants. Superfoods Reference Book lists Superfoods that can help with 12 diseases and 9 types of cancer.

http://www.SuperfoodsToday.com/FREE

Table of Contents

Introduction

Hello,

My name is Don Orwell and my blog SuperfoodsToday.com is dedicated to Superfoods Lifestyle.

This book contains Superfoods Pork recipes from my other books. I hope that you will enjoy 100% Superfoods recipes that I prepared for you.

Superfoods Low Carb Dump Meals Recipes

Allergy labels: SF – Soy Free, GF – Gluten Free, DF – Dairy Free, EF – Egg Free, V - Vegan, NF – Nut Free

Broths

Some recipes require a cup or more of various broths, vegetable, beef or chicken broth. I usually cook the whole pot and freeze it in one cup or half a cup chunks.

Beef Broth

Ingredients

- 4-5 pounds beef bones and few veal bones
- 1 pound of stew meat (chuck or flank steak) cut into 2-inch chunks
- Olive oil
- 1-2 medium onions, peeled and quartered
- 1-2 large carrots, cut into 1-2 inch segments
- 1 celery rib, cut into 1 inch segments
- 2-3 cloves of garlic, unpeeled
- Handful of parsley, stems and leaves
- 1-2 bay leaves
- 10 peppercorns

Instructions - Allergies: SF, GF, DF, EF, NF

Heat oven to 375°F. Rub olive oil over the stew meat pieces, carrots, and onions. Place stew meat or beef scraps, stock bones, carrots and onions in a large roasting pan. Roast in oven for about 45 minutes, turning everything half-way through the cooking.

Place everything from the oven in the slow cooker and cook on low for 6 hours. After cooking, remove the bones and vegetables from the pot.

Strain the broth. Let cool to room temperature and then put in the refrigerator.

The fat will solidify once the broth has chilled. Discard the fat (or reuse it) and pour the broth into a jar and freeze it.

Tomato paste

Some recipes (chili) require tomato paste. I usually prepare 20 or so liters at once (when tomato is in season, which is usually September) and freeze it.

Ingredients

- 5 lbs. chopped plum tomatoes
- 1/4 cup extra-virgin olive oil plus 2 tbsp.
- salt, to taste

Instructions - Allergies: SF, GF, DF, EF, V, NF

Heat 1/4 cup of the oil in a skillet over medium heat. Add tomatoes. Season with salt. Bring to a boil. Cook, stirring, until very soft, about 8 minutes.

Pass the tomatoes through the finest plate of a food mill. Push as much of the pulp through the sieve as possible and leave the seeds behind.

Cook in slow cooker for 4 hours on low.
Store sealed in an airtight container in the refrigerator for up to one month, or freeze, for up to 6 months.

Curry Paste

This can be prepared in advance and frozen. There are several curry recipes that are using curry paste and I decided to take the curry paste recipe out and have it separately. So, when you see that the recipe is using curry paste, please go to this part of the book and prepare it from scratch or defrost of you have it frozen. Don't use processed curry pastes or curry powder; make it every time from scratch. Keep the spices in original form (seeds, pods), ground them just before making the curry paste. You can dry heat in the skillet cloves, cardamom, cumin and coriander and then crush them coarsely with mortar and pestle.

Ingredients

- 2 onions, minced
- 2 cloves garlic, minced
- 2 teaspoons fresh ginger root, finely chopped
- 6 whole cloves

- 2 cardamom pods
- 2 (2 inch) pieces cinnamon sticks, crushed
- 1 tsp. ground cumin
- 1 tsp. ground coriander
- 1 tsp. salt
- 1 tsp. ground cayenne pepper
- 1 tsp. ground turmeric

Instructions - Allergies: SF, GF, DF, EF, V, NF

Heat oil in a frying pan over medium heat and fry onions until transparent. Stir in garlic, cumin, ginger, cloves, cinnamon, coriander, salt, cayenne, and turmeric. Cook for 1 minute over medium heat, stirring constantly. At this point other curry ingredients should be added or let cook and freeze.

Healthy Superfoods Casserole Sauce

- 2 beaten eggs
- Salt, pepper
- 1 cup of low-fat Greek yogurt
- 1 Tbsp. olive oil
- 1/2 cup of low fat parmesan or shredded cheddar cheese

Optional:

- 1 tsp of flax seeds meal
- 1/2 tsp. oregano or thyme or any other herbs

Precooked beans

Again, some recipes require that you cook some beans (low carb ones, cannellini beans, mung beans, black beans) in advance. Cooking beans takes around 3 hours and it can be done in advance or every few weeks and the rest get frozen. Soak beans for 24 hours before cooking them. After the first boil, throw the water, add new water and continue cooking. Some beans or lentils can be sprouted for few days before cooking and that helps if you have stomach problems.

Soups

Italian Pork Soup
Serves 6

Ingredients - Allergies: SF, GF, DF, EF, NF

- 1 pound minced pork
- 1 clove garlic, minced
- 4 cups beef broth
- 1 tomato
- 1/2 cup sliced carrots
- 2 cups raw beans
- 2 small zucchini, cubed
- 2 cups spinach - rinsed and torn
- 1/4 tsp. black pepper
- 1/4 tsp. salt

Put all ingredients in slow cooker and cook on low for 8 hours.

Black Bean Soup
Serves 6-8

Ingredients - Allergies: SF, GF, DF, EF, NF

- 1/4 cup coconut oil
- 1 cup Onions, Diced
- 1 cup Carrots, Diced
- 1 cup Green Bell Pepper, Diced
- 3 cup beef broth
- 2 cups raw Black Beans
- 1 tbsp. lemon juice
- 2 teaspoons Garlic
- 2 teaspoons Salt
- 1/2 tsp. Black Pepper, Ground
- 2 teaspoons Chili Powder
- 1 pound cubed pork
- 1 tbsp. tapioca flour
- 2 cups Water

Instructions

Put all ingredients in slow cooker and cook on low for 8 hours.

Kale Cannellini Beans Pork Soup

Serves 4-6

Ingredients - Allergies: SF, GF, DF, EF, NF

- 2 tbsp. each extra-virgin olive oil or cumin oil and coconut oil
- 3 tbsp. chili powder
- 1 tbsp. jalapeno hot sauce
- 2 pounds bone-in pork chops
- Salt
- 4 stalks celery, chopped
- 1 large white onion, chopped
- 3 cloves garlic, chopped
- 3 cups chicken broth
- 1/2 cup diced tomatoes
- 2 cups raw cannellini beans
- 6 cups packed Kale

Instructions

Put all ingredients in the slow cooker and cook for 8 hours on low.

Bean Soup

Serves 6

Ingredients - Allergies: SF, GF, DF, EF, NF

- 2 cups beef broth
- 4 cups water
- 2 cups sliced carrots
- 2 cups raw white beans
- 1 cup sliced celery & 1 cup sliced leeks
- 2 cups sliced onions
- 1/4 tsp. black pepper
- 1 clove garlic, minced, 1 Tbsp. minced ginger, 3 bay leaves
- 1/2 tsp. salt
- 1 pound minced pork

Put all ingredients in slow cooker and cook on low for 8 hours.

Pork Winter Soup
Serves 6

Ingredients - Allergies: SF, GF, DF, EF, NF

- 2 pounds pork pieces
- 1 clove garlic, minced, 1 Tbsp. minced ginger, 3 bay leaves
- 6 cups water
- ½ cup sliced parsley & ½ cup sliced cilantro
- 2 cups sliced carrots
- 1 cup sliced celery
- 1 cup sliced spring onions
- 2 cups sliced onions
- 1/4 tsp. black pepper
- 1/4 tsp. salt

Put all ingredients in slow cooker and cook on low for 8 hours.

Minced Pork & Tomato Soup

Serves 6

Ingredients - Allergies: SF, GF, DF, EF, NF

- 1 pound minced pork
- 1 clove garlic, minced, 1 Tbsp. minced ginger, 3 bay leaves
- 2 cups water
- 2 cups tomato paste
- 3 cups beef broth
- ½ cup sliced parsley
- 2 cups sliced carrots
- 1 cup sliced celery
- 1/2 cups corn and & ½ cups sliced yellow pepper
- 1 cup sliced green beans
- 2 cups sliced onions
- 1/4 tsp. black pepper
- 1/4 tsp. salt

Put all ingredients in slow cooker and cook on low for 8 hours.

Superfoods Salads

Allergy labels: SF – Soy Free, GF – Gluten Free, DF – Dairy Free, EF – Egg Free, V - Vegan, NF – Nut Free

Salad Dressings
Italian Dressing

Serves 1 - Allergies: SF, GF, DF, EF, V, NF

- 1 tsp. olive oil
- lemon
- minced garlic
- salt

Yogurt Dressing

Serves 1 - Allergies: SF, GF, EF, NF

- half a cup of plain low-fat Greek yogurt or low-fat buttermilk
- olive oil
- minced garlic
- salt
- lemon

Occasionally I would add a tsp. of mustard or some herbs like basil, oregano, marjoram, chives, thyme, parsley, dill or mint. If you like spicy hot food, add some cayenne in the dressing. It will speed up your metabolism and have interesting hot spicy effect in cold yogurt or buttermilk.

Salads

Pork, Red Quinoa, Carrot & Pumpkin Salad
Serves 2

Ingredients - Allergies: SF, GF, DF, EF, NF

- 1 cup cooked quinoa mixed with 1 tbsp. chia seeds
- 1/2 cup chopped pumpkin
- 1/2 cup chopped pork meat
- 1/2 cup chopped carrot
- 1/2 cup green peas

Dressing:
- 1 tbsp. olive oil
- 1 tbsp. fresh lemon juice
- pinch of black pepper
- pinch of sea salt
- 1 tbsp. hemp seeds

Instructions: Mix all ingredients.

Grilled Pork, Asparagus & Tomato Salad

Serves 1 - Allergies: SF, GF, EF, NF

• 5oz. of lean Pork Tenderloin grilled or prepared in the skillet.

• Large mixed asparagus and tomato salad with Italian Salad can be as large as you want, but use half a cup of the dressing.

Nutrition Facts

Serving Size 275 g

Amount Per Serving

Calories 231   Calories from Fat 71

	% Daily Value*
Total Fat 7.9g	**12%**
Saturated Fat 1.5g	**7%**
Trans Fat 0.0g	
Cholesterol 99mg	**33%**
Sodium 249mg	**10%**
Potassium 818mg	**23%**
Total Carbohydrates 5.1g	**2%**
Dietary Fiber 2.4g	**10%**
Sugars 2.4g	
Protein 33.6g	

Vitamin A 58%	•	Vitamin C 57%
Calcium 6%	•	Iron 15%

Nutrition Grade B-

* Based on a 2000 calorie diet

Pork & Kale Salad

Serves 2

Ingredients - Allergies: SF, GF, DF, EF, NF

- 1 lb. pork roast
- 2 cups steamed kale

Dressing:

- 1 tbsp. <u>olive</u> oil or <u>avocado</u> oil
- 1 tbsp. fresh lemon juice
- pinch of black pepper
- pinch of sea salt

Instructions: Steam kale, season and place pork roast on top of kale. Slice pork roast and let roast juices mingles with kale for few minutes.

Superfoods Stir Fry Recipes

Allergy labels: SF – Soy Free, GF – Gluten Free, DF – Dairy Free, EF – Egg Free, V - Vegan, NF – Nut Free

Superfoods Stir Fry Marinade

This marinade has 100% Superfoods ingredients and it's great with any meat or fish and even veggies. Sesame oil and sesame seeds are Superfoods, just like ginger, garlic, scallions, black pepper and red hot chili flakes. I personally don't use soy at all and I replaced soy sauce with fish sauce but you can use soy sauce if you want. Red wine is also Superfood rich in anthocyanidins, quercetin and resveratrol.

- 3 tbsp. fish sauce - optional soy sauce
- 2 tsp. sesame oil
- 1 tsp. freshly grated ginger
- 1 garlic clove, diced
- 1/4 cup red wine or chicken broth or both

Optional:
- 1 Tbsp. arrowroot flour - if you want your stir fry thicker
- 1/4 cup chopped scallions
- 1 tsp. chili flakes (adjust for heat)
- 1/2 tsp. ground black pepper

Korean Spicy Stir Fry Marinade

- 3 tbsp. fish sauce - optional soy sauce
- 1 tsp. sesame oil
- 1 tsp. freshly grated ginger
- 1 garlic clove, diced
- 1 tsp. chili flakes or powder (adjust for heat)

Pork, Bok Choy & Celery Stir Fry
Serves 2 - Allergies: SF, GF, DF, EF, NF

- 10 o.z. Lean Pork Tenderloin
- 2 cups Bok Choy
- 1 cup chopped celery
- 1 tsp coconut oil

Marinade pork in a Superfoods marinade. Stir fry drained pork in coconut oil and when it's no longer pink add celery and stir fry for 1 more minute. Add bok choy and stir fry for a minute longer and then add the rest of the marinade and stir fry for one more minute.

Nutrition Facts

Serving Size 574 g

Amount Per Serving

Calories 316   Calories from Fat 39

	% Daily Value*
Total Fat 4.3g	7%
Saturated Fat 1.1g	6%
Trans Fat 0.0g	
Cholesterol 82mg	27%
Sodium 1156mg	48%
Potassium 1314mg	38%
Total Carbohydrates 34.6g	12%
Dietary Fiber 8.8g	35%
Sugars 8.8g	
Protein 34.5g	

| Vitamin A 33% | • | Vitamin C 81% |
| Calcium 9% | • | Iron 30% |

Nutrition Grade A
* Based on a 2000 calorie diet

Pork, Green Pepper and Tomato Stir Fry

Serves 2

Ingredients - Allergies: SF, GF, DF, EF

- 1/2 pound cubed pork
- 1 cup Green Peppers
- 1/2 cup sliced Tomatoes
- 1 tsp. ground black pepper
- 1 Tsp. oil

Instructions
Marinade pork in a Superfoods marinade. Stir fry drained pork in coconut oil for few minutes, add all vegetables and stir fry for 2 more minutes. Add the rest of the marinade and stir fry for a minute. Serve with brown rice or quinoa.

Pork, Red & Green Peppers, Onion & Carrots Stir Fry

Serves 2

Ingredients - Allergies: SF, GF, DF, EF

- 1/2 pound cubed pork
- 1/2 cup chopped Red Peppers
- 1/2 cup chopped Green Peppers
- 1/2 cup sliced onion
- 1/2 cup sliced carrots
- 1 Tsp. oil

Instructions

Marinade pork in a Superfoods marinade. Stir fry drained pork in coconut oil for few minutes, add all vegetables and stir fry for 2 more minutes. Add the rest of the marinade and stir fry for a minute. Serve with brown rice or quinoa.

Pork Fried Brown Rice

Serves 2

Ingredients - Allergies: SF, GF, DF, EF

- 1/2 pound cubed pork
- 1 cup Peppers
- 1/2 cup sliced Carrots
- 1 Tbsp. black sesame seeds
- 1 cup cooked brown rice
- 1 Tsp. oil

Instructions

Marinade pork in a Superfoods marinade. Stir fry drained pork in coconut oil for few minutes, add all vegetables and stir fry for 2 more minutes. Add the rest of the marinade and stir fry for a minute. Stir in brown rice and black sesame seeds.

Pork, Mushrooms & Basil Stir Fry

Serves 2

Ingredients - Allergies: SF, GF, DF, EF

- 1/2 pound cubed pork
- 1 cup sliced mushrooms
- 1/2 cup Basil leaves
- 1/2 cup sliced carrots and cucumbers
- 1 Tsp. oil

Instructions

Marinade pork in a Superfoods marinade. Stir fry drained pork in coconut oil for few minutes, add all vegetables and stir fry for 2 more minutes. Add the rest of the marinade and stir fry for a minute. Serve with brown rice or quinoa.

Pork Liver & Spinach Stir Fry

Serves 2

Ingredients - Allergies: SF, GF, DF, EF

- 1/2 pound cubed pork liver
- 1 cup Spinach Celery
- 1/2 cup sliced Onions
- 1 Tsp. oil

Instructions

Marinade pork liver in a Superfoods marinade. Stir fry drained liver in coconut oil for few minutes, add all vegetables and stir fry for 2 more minutes. Add the rest of the marinade and stir fry for a minute. Serve with brown rice or quinoa.

Pork, Onion & Bok Choy Stir Fry
Serves 2

Ingredients - Allergies: SF, GF, DF, EF

- 1/2 pound cubed pork
- 1/2 cup sliced onions
- 1 cup sliced Bok Choy
- 1/2 cup sliced Chinese Celery
- 1 Tsp. oil

Instructions

Marinade pork in a Superfoods marinade. Stir fry drained pork in coconut oil for few minutes, add all vegetables and stir fry for 2 more minutes. Add the rest of the marinade and stir fry for a minute. Serve with brown rice or quinoa.

Pork, Cabbage & Bok Choy Stir Fry

Serves 2

Ingredients - Allergies: SF, GF, DF, EF

- 1/2 pound cubed pork
- 1 cup sliced Chinese cabbage
- 1/2 cup sliced bok choy
- 1/2 cup sliced red peppers
- 1 Tsp. oil

Instructions

Marinade pork in a Superfoods marinade. Stir fry drained pork in coconut oil for few minutes, add all vegetables and stir fry for 2 more minutes. Add the rest of the marinade and stir fry for a minute. Serve with brown rice or quinoa.

Pork, Scallions & Celery Stir Fry
Serves 2

Ingredients - Allergies: SF, GF, DF, EF

- 1/2 pound cubed pork
- 1 cup sliced scallions
- 1/2 cup sliced onions
- 1/2 cup sliced Celery
- 1 Tsp. oil

Instructions

Marinade pork in a Superfoods marinade. Stir fry drained pork in coconut oil for few minutes, add all vegetables and stir fry for 2 more minutes. Add the rest of the marinade and stir fry for a minute. Serve with brown rice or quinoa.

Pork Liver, Green Beans & Zucchini Stir Fry

Serves 2

Ingredients - Allergies: SF, GF, DF, EF

- 1/2 pound cubed pork liver
- 1 cup sliced Green Beans
- 1/2 cup sliced zucchini
- 1/2 cup sliced Celery and few red chili peppers
- 1 Tsp. oil

Instructions

Marinade liver in a Superfoods marinade. Stir fry drained liver in coconut oil for few minutes, add all vegetables and stir fry for 2 more minutes. Add the rest of the marinade and stir fry for a minute. Serve with brown rice or quinoa.

Pork & Mushrooms Stir Fry
Serves 2

Ingredients - Allergies: SF, GF, DF, EF

- 1/2 pound cubed pork
- 1 1/2 cup sliced mushroom
- 1 cup sliced onions
- 1 Tsp. oil

Instructions

Marinade pork in a Superfoods marinade. Stir fry drained pork in coconut oil for few minutes, add all vegetables and stir fry for 2 more minutes. Add the rest of the marinade and stir fry for a minute. Serve with brown rice or quinoa.

Pork, Cashews & Carrots Stir Fry

Serves 2

Ingredients - Allergies: SF, GF, DF, EF

- 1/2 pound cubed pork
- 1 cup sliced Green Pepper
- 1/2 cup sliced carrots
- 1/2 cup sliced onions
- 1/2 cup cashews
- 1 Tsp. oil

Instructions

Marinade pork in a Superfoods marinade. Stir fry drained pork in coconut oil for few minutes, add all vegetables and stir fry for 2 more minutes. Add the rest of the marinade and stir fry for a minute. Serve with brown rice or quinoa.

Edamame, Asparagus, Pork & Snow Peas Stir Fry

Serves 2

Ingredients - Allergies: SF, GF, DF, EF

- 1/2 pound cubed pork
- 1 cup sliced Asparagus
- 1/2 cup snow peas
- 1/2 cup sliced onions
- 1/2 cup edamame
- 1 Tsp. oil

Instructions

Marinade pork in a Superfoods marinade. Stir fry drained pork in coconut oil for few minutes, add all vegetables and stir fry for 2 more minutes. Add the rest of the marinade and stir fry for a minute. Serve with brown rice or quinoa.

Superfoods Stews, Chilies and Curries

Superfoods Chili
Serves 6

Ingredients - Allergies: SF, GF, DF, EF, NF

- 2 tbsp. coconut oil
- 2 onions, chopped
- 3 cloves garlic, minced
- 1 pound ground pork
- 3/4 pound pork sirloin, cubed
- 1 cup diced tomatoes
- 1 cup strong brewed coffee
- ½ cup tomato paste
- 2 cups beef broth
- 1 tbsp. cumin seeds
- 1 tbsp. unsweetened cocoa powder
- 1 tsp. dried oregano
- 1 tsp. ground cayenne pepper
- 1 tsp. ground coriander
- 1 tsp. salt
- 3 cups cooked kidney beans
- 4 fresh hot chili peppers, chopped

Instructions

Put all ingredients in the slow cooker and cook on low for 4 hours.

Superfoods Goulash

Serves 4-6

Ingredients - Allergies: SF, GF, DF, EF, NF

- 3 cups cauliflower
- 1 pound ground pork
- 1 medium onion, chopped
- salt to taste
- ground black pepper to taste
- garlic to taste
- 2 cups cooked cannellini beans
- 1/2 cup tomato paste

Put all ingredients in the slow cooker and cook on low for 4 hours.

Cabbage Stewed with Meat

Serves 8

Ingredients - Allergies: SF, GF, DF, EF, NF

- 1-1/2 pounds ground pork
- 1 cup beef stock
- 1 chopped onion
- 1 bay leaf
- 1/4 tsp. pepper
- 2 sliced celery ribs
- 4 cups shredded cabbage
- 1 carrot, sliced
- 1/2 cup tomato paste
- 1/4 tsp. salt

Instructions

Put all ingredients in the slow cooker and cook on low for 4 hours.

Pork Stew with Peas and Carrots

Serves 8

Ingredients - Allergies: SF, GF, DF, EF, NF

- 1 cup chopped carrots
- 1 cup chopped onions
- 2 tbsp. coconut oil
- 1-1/2 cups green peas
- 4 cups beef stock
- 1/2 tsp. salt
- 1/4 tsp. ground black pepper
- 1/2 tsp. minced garlic
- 4 pounds boneless pork shoulder

Instructions

Put all ingredients in the slow cooker and cook on low for 6 hours.

Irish Stew

Serves 8

Ingredients - Allergies: SF, GF, DF, EF, NF

- 2 chopped onions
- 2 Tbsp. coconut oil
- 1 sprig dried thyme
- 2 1/2 pounds pork neck
- 3 chopped carrots
- 4 cups chicken stock
- Salt
- Ground black pepper
- 1 bouquet garni (thyme, parsley and bay leaf)
- 1 bunch chopped parsley
- 1 bunch chives

Instructions

Put all ingredients in the slow cooker and cook on low for 6 hours.

Hungarian Pea Stew

Serves 8

Ingredients - Allergies: SF, GF, DF, EF, NF

- 5 cups green peas
- 1 pound cubed pork
- 2 tbsp olive oil or avocado oil
- 2 1/2 tbsp almond flour (optional)
- 2 tbsp chopped parsley
- 1 cup water
- 1/2 tsp salt
- 1 cup coconut milk

Instructions

Put all ingredients in the slow cooker and cook on low for 6 hours.

Beef, Parsnip, Celery Stew
Serves 8

Ingredients - Allergies: SF, GF, DF, EF, NF

- 2 1/2 pounds cubed pork meat
- 2 chopped onions
- 2 chopped carrots
- 2 Tbsp. coconut oil
- 1 sprig dried thyme
- 2 chopped parsnips
- 4 cups beef stock
- Salt
- Ground black pepper
- 1 bouquet garni (thyme, parsley and bay leaf)
- 1 bunch chopped parsley
- 1 bunch chives

Instructions

Put all ingredients in the slow cooker and cook on low for 8 hours.

Kale Pork

Serves 4

Ingredients - Allergies: SF, GF, DF, EF, NF

- 1 tbsp. coconut oil
- 1 pound pork tenderloin, trimmed and cut into 1-inch pieces
- 3/4 tsp. salt
- 1 medium onion, finely chopped
- 4 cloves garlic, minced
- 2 teaspoons paprika
- 1/4 tsp. crushed red pepper (optional)
- 1 cup white wine
- 1 plum tomato, chopped
- 4 cups chicken broth
- 1 bunch kale, chopped
- 2 cups cooked cannellini beans

Instructions

Put all ingredients in the slow cooker and cook on low for 4 hours.

Braised Green Beans with Pork

Serves 2

Ingredients - Allergies: SF, GF, DF, EF, NF

- 2 cups fresh or frozen green beans
- 1 onion, finely chopped
- 2 cloves of garlic, thinly sliced
- 1/2 inch of peeled/sliced fresh ginger
- 1/2 tsp. red pepper flakes, or to taste
- 1 tomato, roughly chopped
- 1 tbsp. coconut oil
- 1/2 cup chicken broth
- Salt and ground black pepper
- 1/4 lemon, cut into wedges, to serve
- 1 pound lean pork

Instructions

Cut each bean in half. Put all ingredients in the slow cooker and cook on low for 4 hours.

Pork, Celery and Basil Stew
Serves 8

Ingredients - Allergies: SF, GF, DF, EF, NF

- 1 cup chopped onions
- 2 Tbsp. coconut oil
- 2 1/2 pounds chopped pork meat
- 1 chopped carrot
- 2 cups beef stock
- 1 cup white wine (optional)
- Salt
- Ground black pepper
- 1 bunch chopped parsley
- 1 cup chopped celery
- 1/2 cup fresh basil

Instructions

Add all ingredients to slow cooker and cook on low for 8 hours.

Meat Stew with Red Beans
Serves 8

Ingredients - Allergies: SF, GF, DF, EF, NF

- 3 tbsp. olive oil or avocado oil
- 1/2 cup chopped onion
- 1 lb lean cubed pork
- 2 tsp. ground cumin
- 2 tsp. ground turmeric (optional)
- 1/2 tsp. ground cinnamon (optional)
- 2 1/2 cups water
- 5 tbsp. chopped fresh parsley
- 3 tbsp. snipped chives
- 2 cups cooked kidney beans
- 1 lemon, juice of
- 1 tbsp. almond flour
- salt and black pepper

Instructions

Put all ingredients in the slow cooker and cook on low for 4 Hrs.

Pork Tenderloin with peppers and onions

Serves 3-4

Ingredients - Allergies: SF, GF, DF, EF, NF

- 1 tbsp. coconut oil
- 1 pound pork loin
- 1 tbsp. caraway seeds
- 1/2 tsp sea salt
- 1/4 tsp ground black pepper
- 1 red onion, thinly sliced
- 2 red bell peppers, sliced
- 2 cloves of garlic, minced
- 1/4-1/3 cup chicken broth

Instructions

Wash and chop vegetables. Slice pork loin, and season with black pepper, caraway seeds and sea salt. Heat a pan over medium heat. Add coconut oil when hot. Add pork loin and brown slightly. Add onions and mushrooms, and continue to sauté until onions are translucent. Add peppers, garlic and chicken broth. Simmer until vegetables are tender and pork is fully cooked.

Fall Pork and Vegetable Stew
Serves 6-8

Ingredients - Allergies: SF, GF, DF, EF, NF

- 2 pounds pork stew meat
- 1 chopped Tomato
- 1 cup green beans
- 1 cup carrots, sliced
- 1/2 cup green peas
- 1 cup Onions, chopped
- 2 teaspoons Salt
- 1 each Garlic cloves, crushed
- 1/2 tsp. Thyme leaves
- 1 each Bay leaves
- 2 cups chicken broth

Instructions

Cut green beans. Place vegetables and pork in crockpot. Mix salt, garlic, thyme, and bay leaf into broth and pour over meat and vegetables. Cover and cook on low for 7 hours.

Slow cooker pork loin

Serves 4-6

Ingredients - Allergies: SF, GF, DF, EF, NF

- 1-1/2 lb pork loin
- 1 cup tomato sauce
- 2 zucchinis, sliced
- 1 head cauliflower, separated into medium florets
- 1-2 Tbs dried basil
- 1/4 tsp ground black pepper
- 1/2 tsp sea salt (optional)

Instructions

Add all of the ingredients to a crock pot.

Cook on high for 3-4 hours or low 7-8 hours.

Pork, Zucchini, Tomato & Corn Stew
Serves 8

Ingredients - Allergies: SF, GF, DF, EF, NF

- 1/2 cups cooked corn (optional)
- 1 cup chopped onions
- 1-1/2 cups sliced zucchini
- 1 cup chopped tomato
- 2 tbsp. coconut oil
- 2 tbsp. chopped garlic
- 2 tsp. salt and 1 tsp. ground pepper
- 4 pounds cubed pork

Instructions

Put ingredients in the slow cooker. Cover, and cook on low for 7 to 9 hours.

Red Peppers Pork Curry

Serves 8

Ingredients - Allergies: SF, GF, DF, EF, NF

- 3 cups sliced red peppers
- 1 cup chopped onions
- 2 tbsp. coconut oil
- 1 cup curry paste*
- 4 pounds chopped pork meat

Instructions

Put ingredients in the slow cooker. Cover, and cook on low for 7 to 9 hours.

Pork White Bean Chili

Serves 8

Ingredients - Allergies: SF, GF, DF, EF, NF

- 2 cups sliced red peppers
- 1 cup chopped onions
- 2 tbsp. coconut oil
- 1 cup uncooked cannellini beans
- 1/4 cup sliced jalapeno peppers (adjust heat to taste)
- 1 cup sweet corn (optional)
- Salt, ground black pepper and ground cumin to taste
- 2-3 cups beef stock
- 4 pounds minced pork meat

Instructions

Put ingredients in the slow cooker. Cover, and cook on low for 7 to 9 hours.

Pork Meat Stew

Serves 8

Ingredients - Allergies: SF, GF, DF, EF, NF

- 2 tomatoes, sliced
- 1 cup chopped onions
- 2 tbsp. coconut oil
- 2 large red peppers, sliced
- 1 bunch chopped parsley
- Salt, ground black pepper and ground cumin to taste
- 1 cup beef stock
- 4 pounds cubed pork meat

Instructions

Put ingredients in the slow cooker. Cover, and cook on low for 7 to 9 hours.

Pork & Zucchini Stew

Serves 8

Ingredients - Allergies: SF, GF, DF, EF, NF

- 2 medium zucchinis, sliced
- 1 cup chopped onions
- 2 tbsp. coconut oil
- 2 sliced tomatoes & 2 yellow peppers, sliced
- 2 Tbsp. chopped rosemary
- Salt, ground black pepper and ground cumin to taste
- 1 cup beef stock
- 4 pounds cubed pork meat

Instructions

Put ingredients in the slow cooker. Cover, and cook on low for 7 to 9 hours.

Cabbage & Mushrooms Pork Stew

Serves 8

Ingredients - Allergies: SF, GF, DF, EF, NF

- 2 cups sliced mushrooms
- 1 cup chopped onions & 1 cup chopped carrot
- 2 tbsp. coconut oil
- 2 cups sauerkraut
- Salt, ground black pepper and ground cumin to taste
- 2 cups beef stock
- 2 pounds ground pork

Instructions

Put ingredients in the slow cooker and mix. Cover, and cook on low for 7 to 9 hours.

Pork Liver Stew

Serves 8

Ingredients - Allergies: SF, GF, DF, EF, NF

- 2 cups chopped onions
- 2 tbsp. coconut oil
- 3 garlic cloves, minced
- 1 grated carrot
- Salt, ground black pepper and ground cumin taste
- 2 cups chicken stock
- 1 cup red wine (optional)
- 1 tsp. turmeric (optional)
- 4 pounds pork liver cut in stripes

Instructions

Put ingredients in the slow cooker. Cover, and cook on low for 7 to 9 hours.

Pork & Green Peas Stew

Serves 8

Ingredients - Allergies: SF, GF, DF, EF, NF

- 2 cups green peas
- 2 cups chopped onions
- 2 tbsp. coconut oil
- 1 cup chopped carrot
- Salt, ground black pepper and ground cumin to taste
- 2 cups beef stock
- 4 pounds Pork meat

Instructions

Put ingredients in the slow cooker. Cover, and cook on low for 7 to 9 hours.

Pork Broccoli

Serves 8

Ingredients - Allergies: SF, GF, DF, EF, NF

- 2 cups chopped onions
- 2 tbsp. coconut oil
- 3 cups broccoli
- Salt, ground black pepper and 1 Tbsp. chopped garlic
- 2 cups beef stock
- 4 pounds Pork roast

Instructions

Put ingredients in the slow cooker. Cover, and cook on low for 7 to 9 hours.

Pork & Leeks

Serves 8

Ingredients - Allergies: SF, GF, DF, EF, NF

- 2 cups chopped carrot
- 2 tbsp. coconut oil
- 3 cups chopped leeks
- Salt, ground black pepper and ground cumin to taste
- 2 cups beef stock
- 4 pounds cubed pork meat

Instructions

Put ingredients in the slow cooker. Cover, and cook on low for 7 to 9 hours.

Cauliflower, Tomato and Minced Pork

Serves 8

Ingredients - Allergies: SF, GF, DF, EF, NF

- 2 cups chopped tomatoes
- 4 cups cauliflower florets
- 2 cups chopped onions
- 2 tbsp. coconut oil
- Salt, ground black pepper and cumin to taste
- 2 bay leaves & 2 Tbsp. chopped garlic & 1 tsp. oregano
- 2 cups beef stock & 1 cup tomato paste
- 4 pounds minced pork

Instructions

Put ingredients in the slow cooker. Cover, and cook on low for 9 hours.

Tuscan Pork & White Beans

Serves 8

Ingredients - Allergies: SF, GF, DF, EF, NF

- 1 cup tomatoes, sliced
- 2 cups chopped onions
- 2 cups kale or spinach
- 2 cups dry navy beans
- 2 tbsp. coconut oil
- Salt, ground black pepper and ground cumin to taste
- 2 bay leaves & 2 Tbsp. chopped garlic
- 2 cups beef stock
- 2 cups water
- 4 pounds pork shoulder meat

Instructions

Put ingredients in the slow cooker. Cover, and cook on low for 9 hours.

Leeks, Mushrooms & Pork Neck Meat
Serves 8

Ingredients - Allergies: SF, GF, DF, EF, NF

- 2 cups mushrooms, sliced
- 2 cups chopped leeks
- 2 tbsp. coconut oil
- Salt, ground black pepper and ground cumin to taste
- 2 bay leaves & 2 Tbsp. chopped garlic
- 4 cups beef stock
- ¼ cup sesame seeds
- ¼ cup chopped spring onions
- 4 pounds pork neck meat

Instructions

Put all ingredients in the slow cooker except spring onions and sesame seeds. Cover, and cook on low for 9 hours. Sprinkle with chopped spring onions and sesame seeds.

Pork, Beet, Carrots & Onions

Serves 8

Ingredients - Allergies: SF, GF, DF, EF, NF

- 2 cups julienned carrots
- 2 medium beets, peeled and sliced
- 2 cups chopped onions
- 2 tbsp. coconut oil
- Salt, ground black pepper to taste
- 2 cups beef stock
- 4 pounds cubed pork
- 2 Tbsp. minced garlic.

Instructions

Put ingredients in the slow cooker. Cover, and cook on low for 8 hours.

Broccoli, Pork & Peppers

Serves 8

Ingredients - Allergies: SF, GF, DF, EF, NF

- 2 cup sliced yellow and orange peppers
- 1 cup chopped onions
- 2 tbsp. coconut oil
- Salt, ground black pepper to taste
- 1 cup beef stock
- 2 pounds pork chops
- 2 pounds pork neck
- 2 Tbsp. minced garlic.
- 2 cups broccoli florets

Instructions

Put ingredients in the slow cooker. Cover, and cook on low for 8 hours.

Okra & Pork Stew

Serves 8

Ingredients - Allergies: SF, GF, DF, EF, NF

- 3 cups sliced okra
- 2 cups chopped onions
- 2 tbsp. coconut oil
- Salt, ground black pepper to taste
- 2 cups beef stock
- 4 pounds pork neck meat
- 5 cloves garlic, halved lengthwise
- 2 sticks celery, chopped

Instructions

Put ingredients in the slow cooker. Cover, and cook on low for 8 hours.

Pork, Black Beans and Cauliflower

Serves 8

Ingredients - Allergies: SF, GF, DF, EF, NF

- 2 cups cauliflower
- 1 cup black beans
- 2 cups chopped onions & 3 carrots - chopped
- 2 tbsp. coconut oil
- Salt, ground black pepper to taste
- 3 cups chicken stock
- 4 pounds pork meat
- 2 Tbsp. minced garlic & 1 tsp. ground cumin

Instructions

Put ingredients in the slow cooker. Cover, and cook on low for 8 hours.

Celery, Carrots & Cauliflower Pork

Serves 8

Ingredients - Allergies: SF, GF, DF, EF, NF

- 2 cup sliced celery
- 2 cups chopped onions
- 2 tbsp. coconut oil
- Salt, ground black pepper to taste
- 2 cups beef stock
- 4 pounds cubed pork meat
- 2 cups chopped carrots
- 2 cups chopped cauliflower
- 2 Tbsp. minced garlic & 3-4 bay leaves (discard after cooking).

Instructions

Put ingredients in the slow cooker. Cover, and cook on low for 8 hours.

Slow Cooked Carnitas

Serves 8

Ingredients - Allergies: SF, GF, DF, EF, NF

- 2 cups chopped onions
- 2 tbsp. coconut oil
- Salt, ground black pepper to taste
- 2 pounds pork shoulder
- 2 pounds pork neck
- 1 Jalapeno pepper, chopped (to taste).
- 2 Tbsp. minced garlic.
- 1 Tbsp. ground cumin.

Instructions

Put ingredients in the slow cooker. Cover, and cook on low for 8 hours.

Bigos- Polish Pork, Venison & Cabbage Stew

Serves 8

Ingredients - Allergies: SF, GF, DF, EF, NF

- 1 cup chopped onions
- 2 tbsp. coconut oil
- Salt, ground black pepper to taste
- 2 pound pork shoulder meat, cubed
- 2 pounds venison meat, cubed
- 3 cups shredded cabbage
- 2 Tbsp. minced garlic
- 1 Tbsp. ground paprika

Instructions

Put ingredients in the slow cooker. Cover, and cook on low for 8 hours.

Pork, Mushrooms & Herbs Stew

Serves 8

Ingredients - Allergies: SF, GF, DF, EF, NF

- 2 cups chopped onions
- 2 tbsp. coconut oil
- Salt, ground black pepper
- 4 pounds pork shoulder
- 3 cups sliced mushrooms
- 1/2 cup each parsley, cilantro and dill
- 2 Tbsp. minced garlic.

Instructions

Put ingredients in the slow cooker. Cover, & cook on low for 8 hours.

Pork Cauliflower Stew

Serves 8

Ingredients - Allergies: SF, GF, DF, EF, NF

- 2 cups chopped onions
- 2 tbsp. coconut oil
- Salt, ground black pepper to taste
- 4 pounds pork neck meat
- 1 cup sliced green onions
- 1 cup chopped carrots
- 2 cups beef broth
- 3 cups cauliflower
- 1 cup sliced tomatoes

Instructions

Put ingredients in the slow cooker. Cover, and cook on low for 8 hours. Sprinkle with sliced green onions.

Pork Broccoli Carrot Stew

Serves 8

Ingredients - Allergies: SF, GF, DF, EF, NF

- 2 cups chopped onions
- 2 tbsp. coconut oil
- Salt, ground black pepper to taste
- 4 pounds cubed pork meat
- 3 cups broccoli
- 2 cups beef broth
- 2 cups sliced carrots

Instructions

Put ingredients in the slow cooker. Cover, and cook on low for 8 hours.

Minced Pork and Veal Stew

Serves 8

Ingredients - Allergies: SF, GF, DF, EF, NF

- 2 cups finely chopped onions
- 2 tbsp. coconut oil
- Salt, ground black pepper to taste
- 2 pounds minced pork and veal each
- 2 cloves garlic, minced
- 2 cups finely chopped celery
- 2 cups finely chopped carrot
- 1 cup beef broth

Instructions

Put ingredients in the slow cooker. Cover, and cook on low for 8 hours.

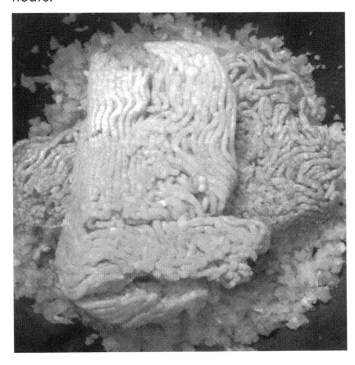

Pulled Pork

Serves 8

Ingredients - Allergies: SF, GF, DF, EF, NF

- 2 cups chopped onions & 2 minced garlic cloves
- 2 tbsp. coconut oil
- Salt, ground black pepper to taste
- 4 pounds pork shoulder
- 1 tsp. dried red pepper flakes (to taste).
- 1/2 cup chicken broth & 1/2 cup apple cider vinegar
- 1 cup tomato paste & 2 tsp. ground cumin
- 1 tbsp. mustard powder & 1 cup tomato paste

Instructions

Put ingredients in the slow cooker. Cover, and cook on low for 8 hours.

Pork, Chinese Celery & Mushrooms Stew
Serves 8

Ingredients - Allergies: SF, GF, DF, EF, NF

- 2 cups chopped onions
- 2 tbsp. coconut oil
- Salt, black pepper to taste
- 4 pounds cubed pork
- 3/4 cup olives.
- 1 cup Chinese celery
- 3 cups sliced mushrooms
- 1 cup beef broth

Instructions

Put ingredients in the slow cooker. Cover, & cook on low for 8 hours.

Pork & Bok Choy Stew
Serves 8

Ingredients - Allergies: SF, GF, DF, EF, NF

- 2 cups chopped onions
- 2 tbsp. coconut oil
- Salt, black pepper to taste
- 4 pounds pork roast
- 1 cup sliced carrots
- 1/4 cup sliced celery
- 3 cups bok choy
- 3 cups beef broth.

Instructions

Put ingredients in the slow cooker. Cover, & cook on low for 8 hours.

Pork, Mushrooms, Red Peppers & Zucchini Stew

Serves 8

Ingredients - Allergies: SF, GF, DF, EF, NF

- 2 cups chopped onions
- 2 tbsp. coconut oil
- Salt, black pepper to taste
- 4 pounds cubed pork
- 3/4 cup sliced carrots
- 2 cups sliced mushrooms
- 1 cup sliced zucchini
- 1 cup sliced red peppers
- 1 cup beef broth

Instructions

Put ingredients in the slow cooker. Cover, & cook on low for 8 hours.

Black Bean Cuban Stew

Serves 8

Ingredients - Allergies: SF, GF, DF, EF, NF

- 1 cup sliced carrot
- 2 cups chopped onions
- 2 red peppers, chopped
- Salt, 1 Tsp. ground cayenne pepper and 1 Tbsp. cumin seeds
- 1 cup corn
- 3 cups dry black beans
- 1 cup tomato paste
- 2 cups beef broth
- 1 tsp. ground coriander
- 4 pounds pork neck meat, cubed

Instructions

Put ingredients in the slow cooker. Cover, & cook on low for 7 to 9 hours.

Plantain Chili

Serves 8

Ingredients - Allergies: SF, GF, DF, EF, NF

- 2 cups sliced plantain (1/2 inch thick)
- 1 cup sliced carrot
- 2 cups chopped onions
- Salt, 1 Tsp. ground cayenne pepper and 1 Tbsp. cumin seeds
- 1 cup corn
- 3 cups dry kidney beans
- 1 cup tomato paste
- 2 cups beef broth
- 1 tsp. ground coriander
- 1/2 cup chopped parsley
- 2 pounds pork neck meat, cubed

Instructions

Put ingredients in the slow cooker. Cover, & cook on low for 7 to 9 hours.

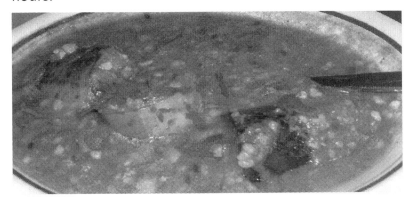

Minced Pork, Tomato & Red Peppers Stew

Serves 8

Ingredients - Allergies: SF, GF, DF, EF, NF

- 1 cup quartered tomatoes
- 1 small chopped onion
- 2 tbsp. coconut oil
- 1 cup chopped red peppers
- Salt, ground black pepper and ground cumin to taste
- 1/4 cup shredded carrots
- 4 pounds minced pork meat

Instructions

Put ingredients in the slow cooker. Cover, & cook on low for 7 to 9 hours.

BBQ Pork

Serves 8

Ingredients - Allergies: SF, GF, DF, EF, NF

- 1/2 cups tomato paste
- 1/4 cup lemon juice
- 2 tbsp. mustard
- 1/2 tsp. salt
- 1/4 tsp. ground black pepper
- 1 tsp. minced garlic
- Salt, 1 Tsp. ground cayenne pepper and 1 Tbsp. cumin seeds
- 4 pounds pork neck meat

Instructions

Put ingredients in the slow cooker. Cover, and cook on low for 7 to 9 hours.

Okra Pork Spinach Stew

Serves 8

Ingredients - Allergies: SF, GF, DF, EF, NF

- 4 cups okra
- 1 sliced carrot
- 1 small chopped onion
- Salt, 1 Tsp. ground pepper
- 1/2 cup sliced tomatoes
- 3 cups spinach
- 1/2 cup tomato paste
- 2 cups beef broth
- 1/2 cup chopped parsley
- 2 pounds pork neck meat, cubed

Instructions

Put ingredients in the slow cooker. Cover, and cook on low for 7 to 9 hours.

BBQ Pork Ribs

Serves 8

Ingredients - Allergies: SF, GF, DF, EF, NF

- 1 cup tomato paste
- 1/4 cup lemon juice
- 2 tbsp. mustard
- 1/2 tsp. salt
- 1/4 tsp. ground black pepper
- 1/2 tsp. minced garlic
- Salt, 1 Tsp. ground cayenne pepper and 1 Tbsp. cumin seeds
- 4 pounds pork ribs

Instructions

Put ingredients in the slow cooker. Cover, and cook on low for 7 to 9 hours. Serve with shredded cabbage.

Pork Shoulder Stew

Serves 8

Ingredients - Allergies: SF, GF, DF, EF, NF

- 3/4 cup sliced red peppers
- 1 sliced carrot
- 1 cup sliced leeks
- Salt & 1 Tsp. ground pepper to taste
- 1 Tbsp. cumin seeds & 3 bay leaves
- 2 cups beef broth
- 2 garlic cloves, minced
- 1 cup beef broth
- 4 pounds pork shoulder

Instructions

Put ingredients in the slow cooker. Cover, and cook on low for 7 to 9 hours.

Mushrooms & Pork Ribs Stew

Serves 8

Ingredients - Allergies: SF, GF, DF, EF, NF

- 2 cups sliced bok choy
- 2 cups sliced mushrooms
- 2 small chopped onions
- Salt & 1 Tsp. ground pepper to taste
- 2 cups beef broth
- 4 pounds pork ribs

Instructions

Put ingredients in the slow cooker. Cover, and cook on low for 7 to 9 hours.

Pork & Cauliflower Stew

Serves 8

Ingredients - Allergies: SF, GF, DF, EF, NF

- 3 cups sliced cauliflower
- 1 cup sliced celery
- 2 small chopped onions
- Salt & 1 Tsp. ground pepper to taste
- 2 cups beef broth
- 4 pounds pork shoulder

Instructions

Put ingredients in the slow cooker. Cover, and cook on low for 7 to 9 hours.

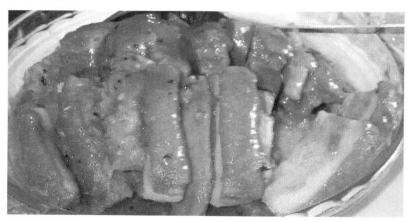

Hong Shao Rou Pork Stew

Serves 8

Ingredients - Allergies: SF, GF, DF, EF, NF

- 1 cup sliced leeks
- 1 sliced carrot
- 2 cups cauliflower
- 1/2 cup chopped green onion
- 1 Tbsp. minced ginger
- Salt & 1 Tsp. ground pepper to taste
- 2 cups beef broth
- 2 Tbsp. fish sauce
- 4 pounds pork belly, cubed

Instructions

Put all ingredients except green onions in the slow cooker. Cover, and cook on low for 7 to 9 hours. Sprinkle with green onions.

Pork Jambalaya
Serves 8

Ingredients - Allergies: SF, GF, DF, EF, NF

- 3 cups diced celery
- 1 sliced carrot
- 2 small chopped onions & 2 cloves minced garlic
- 2 cup sliced mushrooms
- Salt & 1 Tsp. ground pepper to taste
- 3 cups beef broth & 1/4 cup tomato paste
- 1 Tsp. red pepper flakes &
- 4 pounds pork shoulder

Instructions

Put ingredients in the slow cooker. Cover, and cook on low for 7 to 9 hours.

Kimchee Jjiagae – Kimchee Stew

Serves 8

Ingredients - Allergies: SF, GF, DF, EF, NF

- 3 cups kimchee
- 1/2 cup green peas
- 1/4 cup sliced green onions
- 1 small chopped onion
- 1 Tbsp. dried kelp
- 1 cup sliced radish
- Salt & 1 Tsp. ground pepper to taste
- 2 cups beef broth & 1/4 cup Tomato paste
- 1 tsp. red pepper flakes (to taste)
- 3 pounds pork shoulder

Instructions

Put ingredients in the slow cooker. Cover, and cook on low for 7 to 9 hours.

Pork & Red Onions Stew

Serves 8

Ingredients - Allergies: SF, GF, DF, EF, NF

- 1 cup quartered red onions
- 1 sliced carrot
- 2 cups sliced celery
- Salt & 1 Tsp. ground pepper to taste
- 1 cup beef broth
- 4 pounds pork shoulder

Instructions

Put ingredients in the slow cooker. Cover, and cook on low for 7 to 9 hours.

Chanko Nabe Stew

Serves 8

Ingredients - Allergies: SF, GF, DF, NF

- 1 cup Shimeji and enoki mushrooms each (or shiitake)
- 1/2 cup dried kombu seaweed
- Salt & 1 Tsp. ground pepper to taste
- 2 small green onions, sliced & 1 small minced onion
- 1 cup bok choy, sliced
- 2 carrots, sliced
- 2 cups Napa cabbage, sliced
- 2 Tbsp. fish sauce
- 1 Tbsp. miso paste (optional)
- 1 Tbsp. minced ginger
- 5 cups fish broth
- 2 pounds ground pork & 2 eggs for meatballs
- 2 pounds shrimp

Instructions

Make meatballs by mixing 2 pounds ground pork, 1 Tbsp. fish sauce, 2 eggs and minced onion.

Put ingredients in the slow cooker. Cover, and cook on low for 7 to 9 hours.

Szekely Stew

Serves 8

Ingredients - Allergies: SF, GF, DF, EF, NF

- 4 cups sliced sauerkraut
- 2 small chopped onions & 2 cloves minced garlic
- Salt & 1 Tsp. ground pepper to taste
- 1 Tbsp. caraway seeds
- 1 Tbsp. chopped parsley for decoration
- 1 Tsp. red pepper flakes
- 3 Tbsp. sweet paprika
- 4 pounds pork shoulder meat, cubed

Instructions

Put ingredients in the slow cooker. Cover, and cook on low for 7 to 9 hours. Decorate with parsley.

Pork, Green Peppers & Tomato Stew

Serves 8

Ingredients - Allergies: SF, GF, DF, EF, NF

- 2 small chopped onions
- 2 tbsp. coconut oil
- 2 medium tomatoes, chopped
- 2 green peppers, chopped
- Salt, ground black pepper to taste
- 1 cup beef stock
- 4 pounds pork meat, cubed

Instructions

Put ingredients in the slow cooker. Cover, and cook on low for 7 to 9 hours.

Pork Neck and Peppers Stew

Serves 8

Ingredients - Allergies: SF, GF, DF, EF, NF

- 2 small chopped onions
- 2 tbsp. coconut oil
- 2 carrots, chopped
- 1 green pepper, chopped
- Salt, ground black pepper and ground cumin to taste
- 3 cups beef stock
- 1/2 cup chopped parsley & 2 bay leaves
- 1 cup chopped celery
- 4 pounds pork neck meat, cubed

Instructions

Put ingredients in the slow cooker. Cover, and cook on low for 7 to 9 hours.

Pork, Peppers & Green Peas Stew

Serves 8

Ingredients - Allergies: SF, GF, DF, EF, NF

- 2 small chopped onions
- 2 tbsp. coconut oil
- 3 tomatoes, chopped
- 1 red pepper, chopped
- 1 cup green peas
- Salt, ground black pepper and ground cumin to taste
- 1 cups beef stock
- 1 cup sliced celery
- 4 pounds pork, cubed

Instructions

Put ingredients in the slow cooker. Cover, and cook on low for 7 to 9 hours.

Pork Meat & Liver Stew
Serves 8

Ingredients - Allergies: SF, GF, DF, EF, NF

- 1 cup sliced red peppers
- 1 sliced carrot
- 2 small chopped onions & 2 cloves minced garlic
- 1/4 cup vinegar
- Salt & 1 Tsp. ground pepper to taste
- 2 cups beef broth or water
- 1 Tbsp. minced ginger
- 2 pounds pork shoulder, cubed
- 1 pound pork liver, cubed
- 1 pound pork kidney (or pork liver or pork shoulder)

Instructions

Put ingredients in the slow cooker. Cover, and cook on low for 8 hours.

Sauerkraut Pork Stew
Serves 8

Ingredients - Allergies: SF, GF, DF, EF, NF

- 3 cups sauerkraut
- 1/2 cup green peas
- 2 small chopped onions
- 1/2 cup sliced radish
- Salt & 1 Tsp. ground pepper to taste
- 1 cup beef broth & 2 Tbsp. paprika
- 1 tsp. red pepper flakes (to taste)
- 3 pounds pork shoulder

Instructions

Put ingredients in the slow cooker. Cover, and cook on low for 8 hours.

Hunters stew

Serves 8

Ingredients - Allergies: SF, GF, DF, EF, NF

- 1 small chopped onions
- 2 tbsp. coconut oil
- Salt, ground black pepper to taste
- 2 pound pork shoulder meat, cubed
- 2 pounds venison meat, cubed
- 1 cup shredded cabbage
- 2 cups sauerkraut cabbage
- 2 Tbsp. minced garlic
- 1 Tbsp. ground paprika

Instructions

Put ingredients in the slow cooker. Cover, and cook on low for 9 hours.

Pork and Green Peppers stew

Serves 8

Ingredients - Allergies: SF, GF, DF, EF, NF

- 2 medium green peppers, sliced
- 1 medium red peppers, sliced
- 2 small chopped onions
- 2 tbsp. coconut oil
- Salt, ground black pepper and ground cumin to taste
- 2 bay leaves & 2 Tbsp. chopped garlic
- 2 cups beef stock & 2 Tbsp. paprika
- 4 pounds pork shoulder

Instructions

Put ingredients in the slow cooker. Cover, and cook on low for 9 hours.

Superfoods Reference Book

Unfortunately, I had to take out the whole Superfoods Reference Book out of all of my books because parts of that book are featured on my blog. I joined Kindle Direct Publishing Select program which allows me to have all my books free for 5 days every 3 months. Unfortunately, KDP Select program also means that all my books have to have unique content that is not available in any other online store or on the Internet (including my blog). I didn't want to remove parts of Superfoods Reference book that is already on my blog because I want that all people have free access to that information. I also wanted to be part of KDP Select program because that is an option to give my book for free to anyone. So, some sections of my Superfoods Reference Book can be found on my blog, under Superfoods menu on my blog. Complete Reference book is available for subscribers to my Superfoods Today Newsletter. Subscribers to my Newsletter will also get information whenever any of my books becomes free on Amazon. I will not offer any product pitches or anything similar to my subscribers, only Superfoods related information, recipes and weight loss and fitness tips. So, subscribe to my newsletter, download Superfoods Today Desserts free eBook which has complete Superfood Reference book included and have the opportunity to get all of my future books for free.

Your Free Gift

As a way of saying thanks for your purchase, I'm offering you my FREE eBook that is exclusive to my book and blog readers.

Superfoods Cookbook Book Two has over 70 Superfoods recipes and complements Superfoods Cookbook Book One and it contains Superfoods Salads, Superfoods Smoothies and Superfoods Deserts with ultra-healthy non-refined ingredients. All ingredients are 100% Superfoods.

It also contains Superfoods Reference book which is organized by Superfoods (more than 60 of them, with the list of their benefits), Superfoods spices, all vitamins, minerals and antioxidants. Superfoods Reference Book lists Superfoods that can help with 12 diseases and 9 types of cancer.

http://www.SuperfoodsToday.com/FREE

Other Books from this Author

Superfoods Today Diet is a Kindle Superfoods Diet <u>book</u> that gives you 4 week Superfoods Diet meal plan as well as 2 weeks maintenance meal plan and recipes for weight loss success. It is an extension of Detox book and it's written for people who want to switch to Superfoods lifestyle.

Superfoods Today Body Care is a Kindle <u>book</u> with over 50 Natural Recipes for beautiful skin and hair. It has body scrubs, facial masks and hair care recipes made with the best Superfoods like avocado honey, coconut, olive oil, oatmeal, yogurt, banana and Superfoods herbs like lavender, rosemary, mint, sage, hibiscus, rose.

Superfoods Today Cookbook is a Kindle <u>book</u> that contains over 160 Superfoods recipes created with 100% Superfoods ingredients. Most of the meals can be prepared in under 30 minutes and some are really quick ones that can be done in 10 minutes only. Each recipe combines Superfoods ingredients that deliver astonishing amounts of antioxidants, essential fatty acids (like omega-3), minerals, vitamins, and more.

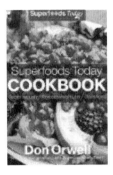

Superfoods Today Smoothies is a Kindle Superfoods Smoothies <u>book</u> with over 70+ 100% Superfoods smoothies. Featured are Red, Purple, Green and Yellow Smoothies

Low Carb Recipes for Diabetics is a Kindle Superfoods <u>book</u> with Low Carb Recipes for Diabetics.

Diabetes Recipes is a Kindle Superfoods <u>book</u> with Superfoods Diabetes Recipes suitable for Diabetes Type-2.

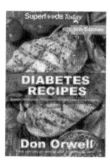

Diabetic Cookbook for One is a Kindle Superfoods <u>book</u> with Diabetes Recipes for One suitable for Diabetes Type-2

Diabetic Meal Plans is a Kindle <u>book</u> with Superfoods Diabetes Meal Plans suitable for Diabetes Type-2

One Pot Cookbook is a Kindle Superfoods <u>book</u> with Superfoods One Pot Recipes.

Low Carb Dump Meals is a Kindle <u>book</u> with Low Carb Dump Meals Superfoods Recipes.

Superfoods Today Salads is a Kindle book that contains over 60 Superfoods Salads recipes created with 100% Superfoods ingredients. Most of the salads can be prepared in 10 minutes and most are measured for two. Each recipe combines Superfoods ingredients that deliver astonishing amounts of antioxidants, essential fatty acids (like omega-3), minerals, vitamins, and more.

Superfoods Today Kettlebells is a Kindle Kettlebells beginner's book aimed at 30+ office workers who want to improve their health and build stronger body without fat.

Superfoods Today Red Smoothies is a Kindle Superfoods Smoothies book with more than 40 Red Smoothies.

Superfoods Today 14 Days Detox is a Kindle Superfoods Detox book that gives you 2 week Superfoods Detox meal plan and recipes for Detox success.

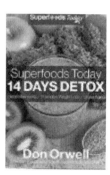

Superfoods Today Yellow Smoothies is a Kindle Superfoods Smoothies book with more than 40 Yellow Smoothies.

Superfoods Today Green Smoothies is a Kindle Superfoods Smoothies book with more than 35 Green Smoothies.

Superfoods Today Purple Smoothies is a Kindle Superfoods Smoothies book with more than 40 Purple Smoothies.

Superfoods Cooking For Two is a Kindle book that contains over 150 Superfoods recipes for two created with 100% Superfoods ingredients.

Nighttime Eater is a Kindle <u>book</u> that deals with Nighttime Eating Syndrome (NES). Don Orwell is a life-long Nighttime Eater that has lost his weight with Superfoods and engineered a solution around Nighttime Eating problem. Don still eats at night☺. Don't fight your nature, you can continue to eat at night, be binge free and maintain low weight.

Superfoods Today Smart Carbs 20 Days Detox is a Kindle Superfoods <u>book</u> that will teach you how to detox your body and start losing weight with Smart Carbs. The book has over 470+ pages with over 160+ 100% Superfoods recipes.

Superfoods Today Vegetarian Salads is a Kindle book that contains over 40 Superfoods Vegetarian Salads recipes created with 100% Superfoods ingredients. Most of the salads can be prepared in 10 minutes and most are measured for two.

Superfoods Today Vegan Salads is a Kindle book that contains over 30 Superfoods Vegan Salads recipes created with 100% Superfoods ingredients. Most of the salads can be prepared in 10 minutes and most are measured for two.

Superfoods Today Soups & Stews is a Kindle <u>book</u> that contains over 70 Superfoods Soups and Stews recipes created with 100% Superfoods ingredients.

Superfoods Desserts is a Kindle Superfoods Desserts <u>book</u> with more than 60 Superfoods Recipes.

Smoothies for Diabetics is a Kindle <u>book</u> that contains over 70 Superfoods Smoothies adjusted for diabetics.

50 Shades of Superfoods for Two is a Kindle <u>book</u> that contains over 150 Superfoods recipes for two created with 100% Superfoods ingredients.

50 *Shades of Smoothies* is a Kindle book that contains over 70 Superfoods Smoothies.

50 *Shades of Superfoods Salads* is a Kindle book that contains over 60 Superfoods Salads recipes created with 100% Superfoods ingredients. Most of the salads can be prepared in 10 minutes and most are measured for two. Each recipe combines Superfoods ingredients that deliver astonishing amounts of antioxidants, essential fatty acids (like omega-3), minerals, vitamins, and more.

Superfoods Vegan Desserts is a Kindle Vegan Dessert book with 100% Vegan Superfoods Recipes.

Desserts for Two is a Kindle Superfoods Desserts book with more than 40 Superfoods Desserts Recipes for two.

Superfoods Paleo Cookbook is a Kindle Paleo <u>book</u> with more than 150 100% Superfoods Paleo Recipes.

Superfoods Breakfasts is a Kindle Superfoods <u>book</u> with more than 40 100% Superfoods Breakfasts Recipes.

Superfoods Dump Dinners is a Kindle Superfoods <u>book</u> with Superfoods Dump Dinners Recipes.

Healthy Desserts is a Kindle Desserts <u>book</u> with more than 50 100% Superfoods Healthy Desserts Recipes.

Superfoods Salads in a Jar is a Kindle Salads in a Jar <u>book</u> with more than 35 100% Superfoods Salads Recipes.

Smoothies for Kids is a Kindle Smoothies <u>book</u> with more than 80 100% Superfoods Smoothies for Kids Recipes.

Vegan Cookbook for Beginners is a Kindle Vegan <u>book</u> with more than 75 100% Superfoods Vegan Recipes.

Vegetarian Cooking for Beginners is a Kindle Vegetarian <u>book</u> with more than 150 100% Superfoods Paleo Recipes.

Foods for Diabetics is a Kindle <u>book</u> with more than 170 100% Superfoods Diabetics Recipes.

Healthy Kids Cookbook is a Kindle <u>book</u> with Superfoods Kids friendly Recipes.

Superfoods Beans Recipes is a Kindle book with Superfoods Beans Recipes.

Diabetic Slow Cooker Recipes is a Kindle book with Superfoods Slow Cooker Diabetic Recipes.

Ketogenic Crockpot Recipes is a Kindle <u>book</u> with Superfoods Ketogenic Crockpot Recipes.

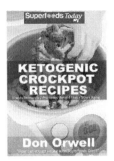

Stir Fry Cooking is a Kindle <u>book</u> with Stir Fry Superfoods Recipes.

Sirt Food Diet Cookbook is a Kindle <u>book</u> with Superfoods Sirt Food Recipes.

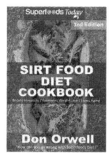

Made in the USA
Middletown, DE
14 November 2022

14950280R00087